National Landmarks

The Washington Monument

by Muriel L. Dubois

Consultant:
Marilyn Harper
Historian
National Park Service, Retired
Washington, D.C.

Bridgestone Books
an imprint of Capstone Press
Mankato, Minnesota

Bridgestone Books are published by Capstone Press
151 Good Counsel Drive, P.O. Box 669, Mankato, Minnesota 56002
http://www.capstone-press.com

Library of Congress Cataloging-in-Publication Data
Dubois, Muriel L.
 The Washington Monument/by Muriel L. Dubois.
 p. cm.—(National landmarks)
 Includes bibliographical references (p. 23) and index.
 Summary: Discusses the history of the Washington Monument, its designer, the
 construction of the monument, its location, and its importance to the people of the
 United States.
 ISBN 0-7368-1117-6
 1. Washington Monument (Washington, D.C.)—Juvenile literature. 2. Washington
Monument (Washington, D.C.)—History—Juvenile literature. 3. Washington (D.C.)—
Buildings, structures, etc.—Juvenile literature. 4. Washington, George, 1732–1799—
Monuments—Washington (D.C.)—Juvenile literature. [1. Washington Monument
(Washington, D.C.) 2. National monuments.] I. Title. II. Series.
F203.4.W3 D83 2002
975.3—dc21   2001003299

Editorial Credits
Erika Mikkelson, editor; Karen Risch, product planning editor; Linda Clavel,
 cover designer and interior layout designer; Erin Scott, SARIN Creative, illustrator;
 Alta Schaffer, photo researcher

Photo Credits
Digital Stock, cover, 1, 4, 6, 20
Hulton/Archive Photos, 10
North Wind Picture Archives, 14, 16
Reuters/Larry Downing/Archive Photos, 18
Stock Montage, Inc., 8, 12

1 2 3 4 5 6 07 06 05 04 03 02

Table of Contents

Fast Facts

★ **Construction Materials:** The Washington Monument is made of marble and granite. The marble came from Maryland and Massachusetts. The granite came from Maine.

★ **Height:** The monument is 555 feet, 5 ⅛ inches (169.3 meters) tall. The Washington Monument is one of the tallest stone towers in the world.

★ **Weight:** The monument weighs 90,854 tons (82,423 metric tons).

★ **Flags:** Fifty American flags representing the 50 states surround the monument.

★ **Date Built:** Work on the monument started in 1848. It was completed in 1884. The monument opened to the public in 1888.

★ **Cost:** The Washington Monument cost $1,187,710.

★ **Restoration:** Workers repaired the Washington Monument between 1997 and 2001. The cost was $9.4 million.

★ **Visitors:** Each year more than 1 million people visit the Washington Monument.

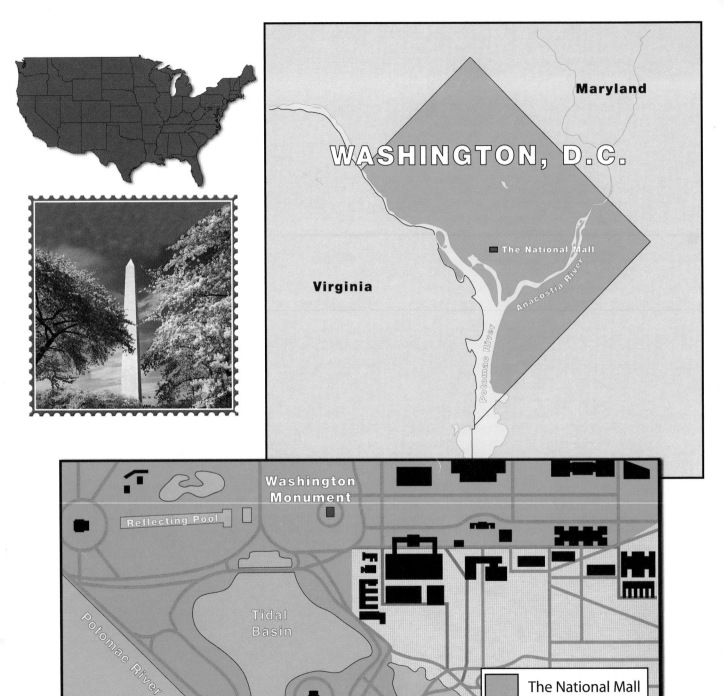

Maryland

WASHINGTON, D.C.

■ The National Mall

Virginia

Anacostia River

Potomac River

Washington
Monument

Reflecting Pool

Potomac River

Tidal
Basin

The National Mall

The Washington Monument

The Washington Monument is a stone obelisk. An obelisk is a tall, four-sided column with a pyramid-shaped top.

The Washington Monument is in the U.S. capital, Washington, D.C. It stands on a small hill. The hill is in the middle of a grassy area called the National Mall. People come to the National Mall to have picnics, play games, and relax. They also visit nearby monuments and museums.

The Washington Monument honors George Washington. He was the first president of the United States. George Washington lived from 1732 to 1799.

Washington was a great war hero before he became president. He led American soldiers against Great Britain in the Revolutionary War (1775–1783). He helped the United States win independence from Great Britain.

The Washington Monument stands in the middle of the National Mall in Washington, D.C.

The Idea for a Monument

After Washington died, one leader suggested that Americans build a tomb for him in the capital. But Washington's family wanted him to be buried at his farm in Mount Vernon, Virginia. People needed to find another way to honor their great leader.

Some Americans wanted to build a statue of Washington on his horse. They thought the statue should stand in their capital city. This city was still being planned at the time.

Americans chose land between Virginia and Maryland for the capital. They named the city Washington, District of Columbia. The capital would not be part of any state.

Pierre Charles L'Enfant drew a plan for the city. The plan showed streets, churches, and fountains. It also included a spot for a monument to Washington.

Americans wanted to honor George Washington with a memorial in Washington, D.C.

Designing the Monument

In 1833, some citizens formed the Washington National Monument Society. Chief Justice John Marshall was the society's president. President James Madison also was a member. The Monument Society raised money for the structure.

The society decided to hold a contest to find a design for the monument. Architect Robert Mills won. He designed many buildings in Washington, D.C.

Mills planned to build a hollow obelisk. He wanted to place columns around the bottom of the obelisk. He drew a statue of Washington and his horse on top of the columns. He also planned to put 30 statues of other Revolutionary War heroes at the site.

The Monument Society liked the design. The work would cost $1 million. The society had only $87,000. They decided to start building the obelisk anyway. They hoped people would donate money. The group chose 30 acres (12 hectares) of land near the spot that Pierre Charles L'Enfant had chosen.

Robert Mills' original design included columns around the bottom of the obelisk.

Workers began the monument in 1848. Leaders held a ceremony on July 4, 1848. President James K. Polk and others gave speeches about Washington.

In 1854, the Monument Society ran out of money. The monument was only 152 feet (46 meters) tall. Congress gave the society $200,000 to continue building.

To help with costs, the society asked each state and territory to donate stones for the monument. They sent marble, granite, and sandstone blocks. Other groups also sent stones. The Pope sent a marble block from Italy. A political party called the Know-Nothing Party stole the block. They wanted only Americans to build the monument.

The Know-Nothings took over the plans. They fired workers who were not born in the United States. The new workers added 26 feet (8 meters) to the monument. The workmanship was poor. Builders later took this work down. The Monument Society took over the project after the Know-Nothing party fell apart.

The unfinished monument stood more than 400 feet (122 meters) shorter than planned.

Work Stops

The Monument Society did not have money to continue work on the Washington Monument. The United States then went to war. The project was put on hold. During the Civil War (1861–1865), people in the North fought against people in the South. Soldiers marched near the unfinished monument. Cows fed on the nearby grass. One man said the monument looked like a broken chimney.

After the Civil War, people wanted to finish the monument. The monument's designer, Robert Mills, had died before the war. Congress and the Monument Society argued. They could not decide how to finish the monument. Some people drew new designs.

The Army Corps of Engineers took over the project. They gave the job to Lieutenant Colonel Thomas Casey. In 1879, he drew new plans for the monument. He checked its base. The base was nearly 20 years old. Casey wanted to be sure it was still strong.

Lieutenant Colonel Thomas Casey changed the original design of the Washington Monument.

Finishing the Monument

Casey continued to work on the monument. Each state and territory had sent a memorial stone. Businesses, clubs, and American Indian tribes also sent stones. Each stone was 4 feet by 2 feet (1.2 meters by .61 meter). In all, Casey had 193 memorial stones for the inside of the obelisk.

Congress voted again to spend $200,000 for the monument. Casey finished the obelisk in four years. Workers put the capstone on the top of the obelisk on December 6, 1884.

President Chester A. Arthur dedicated the monument on February 21, 1885. The celebration ended with a fireworks display.

At first, the only way to get to the top of the monument was to climb 897 steps. In 1888, builders put an elevator inside the monument. Everyone could go to the top more easily. The monument officially opened to the public on October 9, 1888.

On December 6, 1884, the aluminum capstone was placed on the monument.

Changes to the Monument

Today, 50 American flags surround the monument. One flag represents each state.

In 1994, workers put a statue of George Washington in the lobby of the monument. People read facts about George Washington as they wait to go to the top.

In 1992, the National Park Service checked the monument. It needed repair. Some walls leaked. The memorial stones needed cleaning.

In 1997, the Washington Monument was closed to the public. Workers began to restore the monument. They repaired the heating and air conditioning. They put in a new elevator in 1998. They fixed windows. They cleaned the outside marble. They fixed and cleaned the memorial stones inside the obelisk. The National Park Service planned to reopen the Washington Monument by the end of 2001.

Architect Michael Graves designed the scaffolding, or framework, which surrounded the Washington Monument during its restoration.

Visiting the Monument

The Washington Monument is open all year. From April to September, people can visit from 8:00 in the morning until midnight. From October to March, people can visit from 9:00 in the morning to 5:00 in the afternoon. Visitors receive free tickets from the National Park Service.

There is a lot to see and learn at the Washington Monument. The elevator takes visitors to the top of the monument in one minute. There, they can see all of Washington, D.C. National Park Service employees give tours of the monument and tell about the memorial stones.

In the lobby, visitors can view the statue of George Washington. They can learn more about the man this important monument honors.

The Washington Monument is the tallest structure in Washington, D.C.

Important Dates

★ 1791—Pierre Charles L'Enfant maps out Washington, D.C.

★ 1799—George Washington dies.

★ 1836—The Washington National Monument Society holds a design contest. Robert Mills wins.

★ 1848—Work begins on the Washington Monument.

★ 1854—The Monument Society runs out of money. Congress votes to spend $200,000 to finish the monument. Members of the Know-Nothing Party steal a marble block sent by the Pope. The Know-Nothings take over the Monument Society.

★ 1855—Robert Mills dies.

★ 1855–1858—The Know-Nothings add 26 feet (8 meters) of stone to the monument.

★ 1861–1865—The North and South fight the U.S. Civil War. Work stops on the Washington Monument.

★ 1879—Lieutenant Colonel Thomas Casey takes over the plans started by Robert Mills. The Army Corps of Engineers continues building the Washington Monument.

★ 1885—The Washington Monument is dedicated on February 21.

★ 1888—The Washington Monument officially opens to the public on October 9.

★ 1997—The Washington Monument closes for repairs.

Words to Know

architect (AR-ki-tekt)—someone who designs buildings and checks that they are built properly

capstone (KAP-stone)—the highest point of a building or monument

Congress (KONG-griss)—the elected government body of the United States that makes laws

engineer (en-juh-NIHR)—someone who plans and builds machines or structures

obelisk (OB-uh-lisk)—a four-sided post of stone with a top shaped like a pyramid

Pope (POHP)—the head of the Roman Catholic Church

tomb (TOOM)—a grave, room, or building for holding a dead body

Read More

Gilmore, Frederic. *The Washington Monument: A Tribute to a Man, a Monument for a Nation.* Chanhassen, Minn.: Child's World, 2000.

Schaefer, Lola. *The Washington Monument.* Symbols of Freedom. Chicago: Heinemann, 2001.

Useful Addresses

National Park Service
National Capital Region
1100 Ohio Drive SW
Washington, DC 20242

Washington Monument
900 Ohio Avenue SW
Washington, DC 20024-2000

Internet Sites

Monuments and Memorials—The Washington Monument
http://ns.kreative.net/cooper/TourOfDC/monuments/
    washington-monument
Stones and Mortar—The National Mall
http://www.nps.gov/nama/mortar/mortar.htm
Washington Monument
http://www.nps.gov/wamo

Index